DISCOURSE ON THINKING

MARTIN HEIDEGGER

DISCOURSE
ON THINKING

A Translation of *Gelassenheit*

by

JOHN M. ANDERSON and E. HANS FREUND

With an Introduction by

JOHN M. ANDERSON

HARPER ⬤ PERENNIAL

NEW YORK ● LONDON ● TORONTO ● SYDNEY

DISCOURSE ON THINKING

First HARPER COLOPHON edition published 1969 by Harper & Row, Publishers, Inc., New York, N.Y. 10022.

ISBN: 0-06-131459-5

Originally published by Verlag Günther Neske, Pfullingen, under the title Gelassenheit, *copyright © 1959 by Verlag Günther Neske.*

16 RRD(C) 50 49 48 47

CONTENTS

CONTENTS

PREFACE

Martin Heidegger's *Discourse on Thinking*,[1] which is translated here, was published in 1959. It comprises a statement of the point of view of his later thought. Since Heidegger's later thought has evoked so much interest among philosophers and, in the last few years, theologians, it seems important to have significant examples of it available in English. *Discourse on Thinking* is a particularly good example for this purpose not only because it is so recent, but because of its format and style.

Discourse on Thinking has two parts: a Memorial Address in honor of the German composer, Conradin Kreutzer, which Heidegger delivered to a general audience, and a dialogue—or conversation—in which the theme stated in the address is developed in a more specialized and profound way. The dialogue was written from more extended notes on a conversation dating from 1944—45 between a teacher, a scientist, and a scholar.

The work provides an introduction to the later thought of Martin Heidegger, an introduction via his conception of meditative thinking, which is easily intelligible as it is expressed in the Memorial Address. The Memorial Address

1. Martin Heidegger, *Gelassenheit* (Pfullingen: Günther Neske Verlag, 1959).

formulates Heidegger's concern for meditative thinking, without elaborating the details of its fundamental nature. Nonetheless the Memorial Address makes clear Heidegger's understanding of the relation of meditative thinking to contemporary human life, and it states his claim that such thinking has a most important part to play in our life today. In addition, the style of the Address is clear, there is no technical terminology, and the Address has a poetic tone which conveys the high seriousness of the subject.

Further, the explanatory Conversation provides a transitional introduction into the complexities of Heidegger's philosophy. It does so by virtue of being a conversation: the characters of the protagonists can be seen in relation to the ideas they are discussing, the goal of the enterprise is reflected in the attitudes of the speakers, and the free and poetic tone of the speech emphasizes the human significance of the undertaking. This is not to say that the Conversation is easily understood, for it is not. But the reader will be able to see why Heidegger's undertaking is important, and will be able to appreciate why the fulfillment of this undertaking is so extraordinarily difficult.

Those well versed in the intricacies of Heidegger's thought may find the Conversation a refreshingly concrete presentation of one of the fundamental points in his philosophy. The interplay of thought and argument, the free use of word and metaphor, the poetic summaries, all offer a new perspective on an abstract argument, which should be of help in rounding out an awareness of the vision Heidegger has of the place of man in Being. And for the philosopher or theologian as yet unacquainted with Martin Heidegger's thought, the Memorial Address and

Conversation might well provide a tempting taste of a philosophy which already has a place in history.

We wish to acknowledge our indebtedness to Professor Glenn Gray for many valuable suggestions which have materially improved the translation. We thank him for these and for much other help in this enterprise. We are indebted to the Central Fund for Research of The Pennsylvania State University for grants which made possible the completion of this work.

JOHN M. ANDERSON
E. HANS FREUND

INTRODUCTION

There are many who resist a certain kind of philosophy.
They find it hard to enjoy, abstract, and apparently of no
great practical value. It seems to them vague and obscure
nonsense. There have always been such people in the various epochs of human history, just as there have always been
those who find the revelations of speculative thinking to be
of utmost importance. In early Hindu thought, for example,
the contrast between the beast fable and the Upanishads reflects this difference in outlook. The beast fables of the
Panchatantra describe and point up a science of survival, a
hard calculative view of life and its possibilities, and an
unsentimental evaluation of its content:

> Make friends, make friends, however strong
> Or weak they be:
> Recall the captive elephants
> That mice set free.

How sharply such admonitions contrast with the mystical
messages of the Upanishads! How clear they are in formu-
lating the problems and methods of human survival, by
casting them in the terms of animals and their ways—
and how opaque and obscure are the Upanishads in their
unremitting efforts to reveal the ultimate nature of things:

> The knowing Self is not born, it dies not; it sprang
> from nothing, nothing sprang from it.

The same split occurs in early Greek thought. Aesop's fables present to us the lessons in calculation which are the points of the Panchatantra; but the myths and tales of Hesiod's *Theogony* have another both more obscure and more fundamental point to make.

It is this age-old difference in outlook which forms the basis for Martin Heidegger's Memorial Address in honor of the German composer Conradin Kreutzer. Heidegger finds the outlook of the beast fables represented in modern society by the calculative thinking of contemporary science and its applied disciplines. Here is the clear realism of animal life, the sharp and realistic view, the unsentimental outlook quick to take advantage of circumstances to attain an end. With this Heidegger contrasts another kind of thinking which he calls meditative, and which, he says, is implicit in man's nature. It is evident that he finds meditative thinking a difficult and cryptic enterprise, even if it is also one of which every man is capable. Indeed, one of the exhortations of his Address is to inspire us with the courage and persistence that are necessary to think in this way. And he would also make evident to us that to think in this way requires two attributes not at all common, two stands which man can take, and which he calls *releasement toward things* and *openness to the mystery*.

Heidegger relieves somewhat the cryptic character of these attributes by showing their relevance to human life— by showing that man's integrity, his autochthony, depends upon such thinking. By this insistence he also drives home the importance of such thinking to man's very being, claiming, indeed, that even the ultimate meaning of the calculative thinking of modern science and its humanly significant applications are discerned in and through meditative thinking. But fundamentally Heidegger is urging his hearers and readers toward a kind of transmutation of themselves, toward a commitment which will enable them to pass out of their bondage to what is clear and evident but shallow, on to what is ultimate, however obscure and difficult that may be.

Whatever the difficulty of Heidegger's enterprise and of its goal, the difficulty of carrying a reader toward it is not increased in the Memorial Address or the explanatory Conversation by technical terminology or philosophical jargon. It is true that Heidegger is notorious for the use of coined words and phrases, and in many of his writings this in itself makes a grasp of his goal difficult. It is true also that Heidegger often illustrates his points by reference to earlier works in the history of philosophy and to earlier thinkers in complex and original ways, something which makes many of his essays and books uncommonly involved, even by philosophical standards. Yet in the Memorial Address and in the dialogue that develops its theme, Heidegger has chosen a different approach. There are almost no technical or coined terms; indeed, there are essentially only three, translated here as *releasement, in-dwelling,* and *that-which-regions*. Since these words are so integrally connected with the goal of the Address and the dialogue, one may say that their meaning is made clear by the context as a whole (or that the context fails to make their meaning clear). In any case, the peculiarity of the words is not a bar to understanding and participating in Heidegger's enterprise, for the words only sum up and stand for the whole of what is being said, which is to be grasped on the basis of the entire presentation. That is, we should come to see the meaning of these special words as we are led toward the goal Heidegger sets for us.

How does Heidegger lead us toward the transmutation of man he desires, if not by making extensive use of technical terminology as in his earlier works? He does it, in part, by using a language that is simple and has the flavor of the earth. He strives for simile and metaphor involving the soil and growth, and by this means he achieves a poetic tone. Not that his sentence structure or paragraph organization is poetic, for it is not; but phrases and words occurring in the larger context often evoke overtones of feeling associated with the land, with fields, and with what is the ground of things.[1] There is, then, no veil of words standing between the audience and Heidegger's conception of man's authentic nature; rather, words are used with the directness of reference which only poetic handling can achieve. Yet the Address and dialogue are not especially easy to follow, although the former is much simpler than the latter. Actually, Heidegger writes in the manner and with the poetic tone of the mystics, as for example Meister Eckhart to whom he refers. Thus his enterprise might be conceived as similar in difficulty to the task of the mystics who, by an extraordinary and poetic use of words, want to take us with them beyond the ordinary and the familiar, to what is ultimate.

1. For Heidegger's views on language and its function cf. *Was ist Metaphysik?* pp. 50 ff. (Frankfurt a.M.: Klostermann, 1929, 8th ed. 1960), and *Unterwegs zur Sprache* (Pfullingen: Günther Neske, 1959).

This raises the question of whether Heidegger's methods, typical of his later writings, provide a better method for dealing with the ultimate than is to be found in his earlier writings, particularly in *Being and Time*. It is often claimed that Heidegger in *Being and Time* failed to accomplish what he intended. But what did he intend? The amount of technical terminology that must be mastered if we are to judge whether the enterprise projected in *Being and Time* succeeds or not is very great. Fortunately, such mastery is not essential to an understanding of the outlines of the enterprise itself. Indeed, Heidegger states the nature of the enterprise succinctly in the first pages of this work:

Do we in our time have an answer to the question of what we really mean by the word "being"? Not at all. So it is fitting that we should raise anew *the question of the meaning of Being*. But are we nowadays even perplexed at our inability to understand the expression "Being"? Not at all. So first of all we must reawaken an understanding for the meaning of this question. Our aim in the following treatise is to work out the question of the meaning of *Being* and to do so concretely.[2]

Evidently, Heidegger intends to reawaken modern man to the significance of the nature of Being, and to provide an account of its nature. This is a bold enterprise, and one which belongs in the mainstream of Western philosophy.

Those who have read *Being and Time* will remember that one of its major themes is the claim that the traditional approaches to Being have failed; that the conception of Being as a generic object, as beyond experience, has misled philosophical efforts to grasp its nature. In *Being and Time*, by contrast with that tradition, Heidegger follows a method

2. *Being and Time* (Tübingen: Niemeyer, 1929), English translation by Macquarrie and Robinson (New York: Harper & Row, 1962), p. 1.

that begins with man and claims to proceed from his authentic *existence* to an understanding of Being. If a rich and complex analysis may be stated in a few sentences, one might say that Heidegger's method is to develop, first, an account of experience which discloses man as that being for whom his own being is at stake. He then proceeds to show that such a being as man is through and through temporal. Finally, he adumbrates an account which would lead from time to Being. To restate this analysis of experience: when and to the extent that man comes to define himself as aware that his own being is at stake, he comes to authentic existence as temporal; and, as authentic, takes a place in and comprehends Being.

The analysis of experience in *Being and Time* which is directed toward this end uses what is called the phenomenological method, that is, it elicits from a variety of experiences certain pervasive structures of experience. These pervasive structures are, to use the Kantian term, transcendental, or, as Heidegger calls them, ontological; that is, they structure all of experience. Such structures ultimately reveal the temporal ground of man's being; as, for example, the structures called *being toward death* and *resolve* do, when we come to see that in them man is actively engaged in caring.

The question we must ask next is whether a method eliciting man's temporal being in the terms of these transcendental structures enables Heidegger to carry out his enterprise and to formulate the nature of Being. As has been indicated, many readers of *Being and Time* have found the enterprise incomplete and incompletable. Logically, the difficulty standing in the way of completion seems to be that the transcendental structures of experience which Heidegger elicits are formulated as static and final. These structures provide a grasp of man's being as temporal; but because they are the structures of man's experience, they can do this in a limited way only. These structures constitute the horizons of human awareness, and a method which explicitly formulates them extends our understanding beyond the contents of awareness to its deeper nature as such. The formulation of the horizons, the conditions of awareness, reveals man as temporal; but such a formulation reveals this solely as man sees it, solely in human terms. There is in such a method an ineluctably subjective orientation which must characterize its results. Thus it seems impossible to escape from subjective distortions and to learn anything about Being as such by means of the method Heidegger used in *Being and Time*. What seems to be necessary in order to comprehend Being is a method of understanding which can grasp man's nature as temporal in terms of its ground, rather than simply in terms of the horizons of experience. Such a method could reveal man's temporality in relation to what was beyond man, and not merely in the terms of man himself.

But there is circumstantial as well as logical evidence for believing that the enterprise of *Being and Time* remains incomplete. We know, for example, that Heidegger outlined this work, initially, to include material not published in the book, although it is probable that it was written. *Being and Time* as published consists of but a part of a longer projected study. We know what the unpublished parts of this study were intended to contain, for we have Heidegger's word on the matter. In part, the projected but unpublished sections of the book were to have dealt with an analysis of the history of philosophy; and in part they were to have included an account of the relation between Time and Being. In this last part, it seems clear, the problem of how Being could be seen in relation to man's being as temporal was to have been discussed explicitly and, presumably, solved. That is, Heidegger's claim that Being can be disclosed along a path beginning in man's authentic existence, which is fundamentally temporal, was to have been justified by showing the way to Being. That this part of the book has not yet been published, and that in the years immediately following the publication of *Being and Time* none of Heidegger's writings offers the solution, constitutes historical evidence that the method and categories of *Being and Time* were somehow inadequate to deal with the problem effectively. Heidegger himself says of this part:

The adequate reproduction of and participation in this other thinking that leaves subjectivity behind is indeed rendered difficult by the fact that when *Being and Time* was published, the third Division of the first Part, entitled "Time and Being" was held back. . . . The Division in question was held back because thinking failed in adequately articulating this turn, and did not achieve its goal by means of the language of metaphysics.[3]

This view is supported also by the fact that the book, *Introduction to Metaphysics*,[4] published some years after *Being and Time*, deals with the problem of Being, but from a quite different direction. Where one might have supposed that the later book would be a completion of the

3. *Über den Humanismus* (Frankfurt a.M.: Klostermann, 1949), p. 178. There is evidence that a new formulation of "Time and Being" exists and will eventually be published.

4. *An Introduction to Metaphysics*, English translation by Ralph Manheim (Yale University Press, 1959).

enterprise begun earlier, it seems to be an independent in-
quiry, or at least an experiment in a new approach. To
define this different approach Heidegger asks again the
traditional question: Why does something exist, rather
than nothing? Evidently an answer to this question would
reveal something about the nature of Being, since it would
reveal the relation of particulars to their ground. Yet while
Heidegger's efforts to answer this ultimate question are almost as interesting as the question, they can not be said to
have provided the answer. What he does is to present an
illuminating criticism of European philosophy. In this
criticism, he shows how the tradition of European philosophy has concerned itself with an analysis of the opposites
of Being, such as becoming, appearance, and so on, and
then has tried to transcend these opposites to arrive at Being. And he, by contrast to this sophisticated approach,
offers the suggestion that a return to the naïve but un-
distorted intuition of Being in the earliest Greek philosophers could put us on the right path. But it is not very
clear in the *Introduction to Metaphysics* what this path
could be.

When we turn to Heidegger's later writings, for example the Memorial Address and Conversation which follow, we must view them in the light of the uncompleted
enterprise formulated in *Being and Time*. We should ask,
first, whether the enterprise is in general the same as the
earlier one. If it is the same, we should ask, second, whether
the methods used and the orientation to the problem are
similar. Third, and finally, of course, we want to know
whether the enterprise has at last succeeded.

In the Memorial Address in honor of Conradin Kreutzer,

Heidegger seeks to show his audience that it is time to re-
new the search for a new ground of meaning, and that the
sense of the importance of such a ground of meaning has
been overlooked in the modern world where applied science
and calculative thinking dominate our lives. He calls upon
us to reawaken to a task we have forgotten, and to under-
take this task, however arduous it may be. He goes so far
as to suggest that if this task is undertaken, it might be
completed. The interesting thing in this analysis is that if
the phrase "new ground of meaning" is substituted for the
word "Being" in the passage quoted from *Being and Time*
on page 15 above, the enterprise formulated in the Memorial Address and that in *Being and Time* would be exactly
the same. Indeed, the enterprise of reawakening an awareness of the significance of Being, and of determining the
nature of Being, seems characteristic of both the earlier and
the later Heidegger. This answers our first question.

But that answer raises the second question: Is the method
in these later writings the same as in the earlier ones? It
has been noted already that the answer to this question is
partially negative, at least. For it has been noted that
Heidegger's use of language is markedly different in his
later writings, and particularly in those translated here.
Here he does not rely upon technical terminology, but upon
poetic directness. However important this is, it is not the
whole story; and there is at least one sense in which Heidegger's method in the Memorial Address and the Conversation
is the same as in his earlier writings. In the Memorial
Address it is claimed that man's nature includes the capacity for meditative thinking, and that the proper exercise of
this capacity, difficult though it is in terms of releasement

toward things and openness to mystery, can lead to a new ground of meaning. This is the claim that man's nature provides the basis through which one wins an understanding of Being. Clearly, this is the method of *Being and Time* carried over. It is interesting to observe in this connection that the method of the Conversation is the same, for there each stage in the approach to Being depends upon the development of a stage in the nature of thinking, which is man's nature. In a very general way, then, the approach in *Being and Time* to Being, and in the Memorial Address and the Conversation to a new ground of meaning, is the same. Yet this similarity must not remain unqualified, for Heidegger himself has said:

I have forsaken an earlier position, not to exchange it for another, but because even the former position was only a pause on the way. What lasts in thinking is the way.[5]

In this reference to his earlier thought, Heidegger clearly indicates that there has been a major change. Yet, if the nature of Being is still the end at which thought aims, and if thought is still conceived as moving toward this end through man, in what does the change consist?

The Memorial Address and the Conversation which develops its theme reflect this change in the conception of the defining character of man's nature. In *Being and Time* this character is understood as the transcendental structure of experience. But in the Memorial Address and the Conversation, as in other later works, this character is understood quite differently. How, then, is it conceived there? It is conceived as the way in which man is involved immediately

5. *Unterwegs zur Sprache* (Pfullingen: Günther Neske, 1959), pp. 98 ff.

and directly in Being. Some aspects of this new understanding are evident in the Conversation. First, the Conversation begins with a cryptic statement of this new conception attributed to the Teacher, who says that ". . . the question concerning man's nature is not a question about man."[6] This seems to be a paradoxical statement, and yet the suggestion is that the development of this idea is to be a theme of the subsequent discussion. Implied in this claim, that man's nature is to be found in relation to something else, is a suggestion that to comprehend man one must transcend the specifically and merely human, the subjective.

Heidegger expresses this claim metaphorically by placing the Conversation "far from human habitation." It is worth noting that the Conversation begins at a distance from what is merely human, and that it is terminated at a point where the participants once again approach human habitation: the symbolic significance should not be missed. But, third, Heidegger also develops this claim explicitly in a number of ways. For one example, consider the nature of *waiting* as it is analyzed in the Conversation. Waiting is a human activity, of course; but Heidegger wants to show that it has a deeper significance and involves a reference beyond the merely human, the subjective. Normally, when we wait we wait *for* something which interests us or which can provide us with what we want. When we wait in this human way, waiting involves our desires, goals, and needs. But waiting need not be so definitely colored by our nature. There is a sense in which we can wait without knowing for what we wait. We may wait, in this sense, without waiting for anything; for anything, that is, which could

6. "Conversation," p. 58 below.

be grasped and expressed in subjective human terms. In this sense we simply wait; and in this sense waiting may come to have a reference beyond man. The difference between these two kinds of waiting may be expressed by saying that when we wait in a merely human way we wait *for*, whereas in the deeper sense of waiting we wait *upon*. The different prepositions are intended to refer in the case of "for" to subjective human expectations of some sort, but in the case of "upon" to what is, if given, a gift. As Heidegger says: "In waiting [upon] we leave open what we are waiting for."[7] This is to say that man's true nature may relate directly to what transcends him, however difficult it may be to state this in ordinary terms. In the context of the Conversation, this possible transcendence, which is found in man's true nature, is developed as a transcendence to Being.

Yet one may object that while an analysis of waiting into two kinds is suggestive, it is hardly conclusive in showing that the movement from man to Being can be made if the correct path is discerned. Waiting *upon* does not evoke Being, even though the suggestion is that if anything responded to such waiting, it would be Being. Let us, therefore, consider another aspect of the relation of man to what transcends him. The comprehension of meditative thinking as a structure of man relating directly to Being is clearly the central theme of the Address and Conversation. Of course, thinking is peculiarly human; but it is human in at least two senses. The traditional and usual view of thinking sees it as the representing of what is typical of things; that is, as a kind of human activity leading to an understanding

7. "Conversation," p. 68 below.

of objects. In this sense it is a kind of willing, and so to be seen as something specifically and merely human. At one extreme this is what Heidegger calls calculative thinking, which is characterized by human methods of approaching things, and by the fact that in calculative thinking we deal with things in our terms for our advantage. Yet there is a second sense of thinking, analogous to the second sense of waiting, in which thought refers beyond the human, transcends reference to human affairs: this is meditative thinking.

Thinking of this second sort does exist. It is to be found, for one example, throughout the whole Conversation. And such thinking has a content, it is about something. To begin to comprehend what is involved in this kind of thinking, we may observe, somewhat negatively, that it does not represent, that it does not construct a world of objects. By contrast to representative thinking, it is thinking which allows content to emerge within awareness, thinking which is open to content. Now thinking which constructs a world of objects understands these objects; but meditative thinking begins with an awareness of the field within which these objects are, an awareness of the horizon rather than of the objects of ordinary understanding. Meditative thinking begins with an awareness of this kind, and so it begins with content which is given to it, the field of awareness itself.

When viewed from within, as by a practitioner, for example, certain properties of meditative thinking may be discerned. Indeed, one of these properties has just been pointed out. Meditative thinking is thinking which is open to its content, open to what is given. A man engaged in meditative thinking might well characterize what he was doing as being open; that is, he might comprehend meditative thinking as a fundamental property of human nature, the property of openness. Yet such thinking does not involve what is ordinarily called an act of will; for one does not will to be open. Quite the contrary, meditative thinking involves an annulling of the will. Yet, such thinking is not a passive affair either; clearly, man does not come to be open through indifference or neglect. To be open is difficult for man. Since openness involves meditative thinking, it is suggestive to speak of this thinking as a higher kind of activity than willing. But perhaps the real point is that this kind of thinking lies, as Heidegger says, ". . . beyond the distinction between activity and passivity. . . ."[8]

Let us regard meditative thinking, then, as a higher kind of activity than is involved in the exercise of any subjective human power. We might think of it, metaphorically, as the activity of walking along a path which leads to Being. Certainly metaphorically, the conversation along the path referred to in the Conversation symbolizes such an activity and such a direction. In any case, this higher activity of thinking in relation to the openness involved in it is so important that it needs a special name. Heidegger calls it *releasement*. Releasement is a defining characteristic of man's true nature involving openness and, through it, direct and immediate reference beyond man to Being.

Releasement involves openness, but it would be misleading to suppose that that involvement is adequately sketched by the relatively simple account of the preceding paragraphs. One goal of the Conversation is to provide a developing comprehension of releasement as it involves and is

8. "Conversation," p. 61 below.

involved in Being. In consequence, for example, Heidegger speaks of two aspects of releasement, the first of which is being released *from*, and the second, authentic releasement, may be described as being released *to*.[9] Again, for another example, releasement has hidden in it, he says, a kind of steadfastness which is related to a resolve for truth, and which when fully comprehended is to be called "in-dwelling."[10] Meditative thinking is not a simple opening to Being, as the nature of authentic releasement (releasement *to*) might suggest, for it involves a resolve in regard to Being. In meditative thinking, man opens to Being and resolves for its disclosure. Such a resolve is not an exercise of subjective human powers; rather, it is taking a stand which reveals Being, a kind of dwelling in Being. This inner nature of releasement must be considered later in this introduction; it is mentioned here only to emphasize the complexity of the relation of releasement and openness.

The defining character of man's nature (meditative thinking), then, is conceived in the Conversation in a way radically different from that in *Being and Time*. The transcendental structure of experience analyzed in *Being and Time* in such terms as *being-in-the-world*, *being-toward-death*, and *temporality* is replaced in the Conversation by an analysis of the higher activity of meditative thinking which involves Being directly. The intention of this change is revealed as a deliberate effort of Heidegger to assure the possibility of moving through man to Being. There is no doubt that Heidegger believes this to be possible in the terms of meditative thinking, for he does not

9. "Conversation," p. 73 below.
10. "Conversation," p. 81 ff. below.

hesitate to speak directly about Being and to give an account of its nature. In the Conversation, however, Heidegger does not use the word *Being;* but in order to stress an inherent openness and activity of Being, he uses the word *region* and its cognates instead. That is, a region is open; moreover, it is possible to designate a region as inherently dynamic by using the phrase *that-which-regions,* and, even further, to use the verb *regioning* to express this activity directly. But let us quote from such a direct account of Being in these new terms to illustrate the point we are making.

The region gathers, just as if nothing were happening, each to each and each to all into an abiding, while resting in itself. Regioning is a gathering and re-sheltering for an expanded resting in an abiding. So the region itself is at once an expanse and an abiding. It abides into the expanse of resting. It expands into the abiding of what has freely turned toward itself. . . .[11]

Now the point is not that these sentences be clear out of context, but that they claim to give an explicit account of Being, of that-which-regions; and that this account has been reached from the starting point of meditative thought, of man's nature.

Three questions were asked above about the characteristics of Heidegger's later thought. The first two have been answered, for we concluded that the goal of his later thought is the same as, but its method different from, that of his earlier thought. Does Heidegger's enterprise, as developed in his later thought, succeed? This was the third question, and it remains before us. It would be impossible in this brief introduction to formulate an answer to such a basic

11. "Conversation," p. 66 below.

question; but the key to its answer can be suggested. The whole of the claim implicit in the account Heidegger gives of Being in the Conversation rests upon the assumption that the analysis of man's nature, as found in meditative thinking, provides the key to a direct approach to Being. Close attention to the nature of this assumption, and to the evidence which Heidegger gives for it, will provide considerable insight into the problem of its justification.

In the Conversation, three kinds of evidence seem to be offered for the justification of this assumption. This evidence amounts to showing that Being as reached through meditative thinking is partly identical with the nature and movement of such thinking. Certainly if this were not so, meditative thinking would be powerless to reach Being. The details given in the Conversation must be studied carefully to understand the point fully, and here a suggestion of the argument and its results must suffice. Fortunately, it is the nature of the evidence, and not its details, which is important for an understanding of Heidegger's general claim. Thus we may observe first that meditative thinking is an opening of man to something, as is emphasized by calling such thinking releasement.

In releasement man is open, that is, is an openness. What then, we may ask, does man open to? In a word, of course, the answer is: to the given. But Heidegger is not content to present this answer, for he wishes to justify the identity he is claiming. To do so, he argues that the given, too, is an openness and, as we shall see, an opening. Meditative thinking characterizes man's true nature, his being, as openness in which he is partly identified with the given. Man becomes partly identified with the given by opening to it as, in turn, the given opens to him.

Let us consider this argument somewhat more carefully. As already noted, meditative thinking involves an awareness of the field of awareness, or, as Heidegger likes to say, an awareness of the horizon of the consciousness of objects. If one comprehends this situation fully, one sees that meditative thinking is an opening to what is beyond the horizon of such knowing. But the possibility of any such opening must depend to some degree upon what lies beyond the horizon, and, indeed, upon the openness of that. To restate the argument: viewed from within, our consciousness of the world of objects is an unbounded field of awareness; viewed from within, this field of awareness has no fixed limits, but only a horizon. In part, meditative thinking consists in becoming aware of the horizon as such, that is, as an opening out and so as standing open. But an awareness of the horizon in this explicit sense as an openness is possible just because the horizon is set within an openness of which it is but one side, as it were. The openness in which the horizon of consciousness is set Heidegger calls the region.

What is evident of the horizon [its openness], then, is but the side facing us of an openness which surrounds us; an openness which is filled with views of the appearances of what to our re-presenting are objects. In consequence the horizon is still something else besides a horizon . . . [and] this something else is the other side of itself, and so the same as itself. You say that the horizon is the openness which surrounds us. But what is this openness as such, if we disregard that it can also appear as the horizon of our re-presenting? It strikes me as something like a *region*. . . .[12]

12. "Conversation," p. 64 ff. below.

That openness of man which is grounded in the openness of the region is but a part of the identity of man and the given of which we are speaking. A more important part of this identity is to be found in a common activity. As we have noted, the openness of man is an opening, a kind of higher activity. The openness of the region which is the ground of man's opening must also be grasped as movement, something which is easier if we name it properly as that-which-regions. The openness of the region is not a vacuum; if it were, it would go unnoticed by man. Man's opening must occur in his awareness of the givenness of the transcendental horizon. As Heidegger says, ". . . the horizon is but the side of that-which-regions turned toward our re-presenting. That-which-regions surrounds us and reveals itself to us as the horizon."[13] Or again, ". . . It seems a region holds what comes forward to meet us; but we also said of the horizon that out of the view which it encircles, the appearance of objects comes to meet us. If now we comprehend the horizon through the region, we take the region itself as that which comes to meet us."[14] The basic sense in which the region is an opening is complex, and is not perfectly stated in these quotations. However, the point being made is just that the region is an opening; that we can and must refer to it as that-which-regions; and that we can refer to its opening as such, that is, to regioning. In the opening of the region, its regioning, we have what supports and manifests itself in part as the opening of man, his meditative thinking.

Now it is true that since that-which-regions is a region-

13. "Conversation," p. 72 ff. below.
14. "Conversation," p. 65 below.

ing, a movement, we can understand man's nature as
brought forth in this movement. That-which-regions is a
dynamic ground in which man's nature emerges. Yet there
is something unsatisfactory if the matter is left here, for
such an account seems to place man and meditative thinking as but a moment in the given development of that-
which-regions: it stresses the identity of man and that-
which-regions. Such an account hardly touches upon the
fact that meditative thinking does not simply occur as a
part of a more inclusive, given development. Clearly, such
thinking is more than an instance of such development;
it also serves to receive the development. The reference
of meditative thinking to that-which-regions as partly identical with man may be seen in releasement as such. In releasement as such, thinking is open to its ground as given.
But the reference of thinking to that-which-regions as re-
ceiver of it may be seen only in what Heidegger calls *in-
dwelling*. As in-dwelling, meditative thinking expresses the
requirement of becoming true for that-which-regions.
Through in-dwelling, man is able to express a resolve for
truth. It is important not to misunderstand this requirement
as a subjective one; for while the resolve for truth is made
by man, what is required by him is independent of him.
Truth is not subjective. Essentially, the resolve for truth
is a requirement that the regioning of that-which-regions
be an unveiling. In such disclosure, man's nature as thinking serves not to create or to impose structure, but for
". . . a receiving of the regioning of that-which-regions."[15] Evidently there is a mutual relation here, for
Heidegger says, ". . . the nature of man is released to

15. "Conversation," p. 81 below.

that-which-regions because this belongs to it so essentially, that without man that-which-regions can not be a coming forth of all natures, as it is."[16] Man is essential to this disclosure.

Clearly, then, the identity noted in man's opening and openness and the opening and openness of that-which-regions expresses only the relation of man to the given, and so is but a partial identity. The relation between man and that-which-regions is much more complex than this, for the sense in which meditative thinking receives and is necessary for the coming forth of all natures is as important as this identity. Thus, to proceed from man's nature to Being, Heidegger needs to produce a second kind of evidence that this is possible. This is the evidence that man's nature as it expresses the requirement of becoming true, the coming forth of all natures, is compatible with that-which-regions and can play a positive part in this respect.

Man, in this sense, is the peculiar being with respect to whom that-which-regions unveils and discloses. This distinction of man, expressed in his resolve for truth, makes him the standard for and the recipient of the disclosure of that-which-regions; man stands out in order to be where that-which-regions unveils. Or, we might say, man, as indwelling, stands within that-which-regions and effectively resolves for its disclosure, its coming forth in truth. But how can this disclosure take place? How is this aspect of man's nature interwoven compatibly with the underlying identity already noted? The difficulty of showing how this is done is just the difficulty of showing how man is brought forth in the regioning of that-which-regions and yet comes

16. "Conversation," p. 83 below.

forth in such a distinctive way—of showing, that is, how it is that man's nature is necessary because of having its ground in the givenness of that-which-regions, and yet is emergent as a nature which resolves for and receives the disclosure of its ground. Heidegger seeks to make the difficult analysis which will clarify this point, first in terms of history, and then in an interesting generalization with respect to truth based upon his interpretation of history.

There is a sense in which, as a consequence of man's resolve for truth, that-which-regions is disclosed in history.[17] To understand this we must observe initially that the process of that-which-regions, its regioning, takes place in two quite different ways. To emphasize this difference, Heidegger refers to this process when it results in things as *determining*, but when it results in man he calls it *regioning with respect to man*. Put in this way, this duality emphasizes man's nature as involved in and involving truth, and contrasts it with the nature of things. Yet Heidegger holds that man's requirement of truth is the basis of the relation of man to things and that this relation occurs as history. To be grasped as functioning in this way, history must be understood in a very fundamental sense, that is, as ". . . a history which does not consist in the happenings and deeds of the world. . . . Nor in the cultural achievements of man."[18] What is fundamental in history is not its obvious sequential character but, rather, historical thinking. Thus ". . . the concept of the historical means a mode of knowing and is understood broadly."[19] From this perspec-

17. For a general account of history see *Identität und Differenz* (Pfullingen: Günther Neske, 1957), p. 64 and elsewhere.
18. "Conversation," p. 79 below.
19. Cf. *Identität und Differenz*, p. 51.

tive we should look for history where the articulation of
the natures of things occurs, as in the evolution of the
subject-object relation or in the sciences understood metho-
dologically. As these examples suggest, such history relates man to things because through it things are sustained
by man's requirement that they become true, for this is a
requirement that the nature of things be brought forth.
Such an articulation, such history, is an aspect of the disclosure of that-which-regions, a disclosure which takes
place in relation to man.

Now history, as a mode of knowing, is a kind of re-
collecting, a returning to origins as well as an articulation
of the nature of things. But it is a return to origins not
merely in the sense of recounting an intelligible story of
development and change. As a mode of knowing, it is a
return to origins in the sense in which intelligibility must
have its roots in what is prior to thought, must abide in
what is the source of all articulation. It is in this most
fundamental sense that history involves a beginning. Historical knowing necessarily has origins which are prior to it,
and it comprises an intelligible expansion which develops
in the terms of these origins.

But what are these origins? We may understand something more about them if we look at the more general
circumstances of the bringing forth of all natures, of which
history is an aspect. To comprehend fully this bringing
forth of all natures, one must observe that for man to resolve for truth and so to serve that-which-regions in this
movement is to set aside subjective demands and pretensions,
to be, in a word, noble. Now nobility connotes heritage and
origins; and suggests, in consequence, that resolving for

truth involves a return to man's origins. This "step back-ward," this return becomes explicit, not in going back to a literal beginning, but in the awareness that thinking as the resolve for truth is grounded.[20] The resolve for truth which expresses that-which-regions as the bringing forth of all natures, is not a subjective expression; rather, it springs from an inner necessity which man can come to understand as the ground of his thinking itself. It is not a necessity forced upon man from without. As an inner necessity it is given to man as a gift, a gift which justifies man in serving that-which-regions as the being for whom the unveiling of that-which-regions occurs. His service in this exalted way is not accident, but a necessity demon-strated by the nature of thinking as having an origin prior to thought. And what is this origin? It is the *nature* of that-which-regions. "In the nature of thinking so understood, we may have found what we seek. . . . This is the *nature* of that-which-regions."[21]

Let us pause briefly to note explicitly that our analysis has led us to the *nature* of that-which-regions. The ground of meditative thinking, as it involves a resolve for truth, is not that-which-regions, but its *nature*. Meditative think-ing, therefore, not only has two aspects corresponding to the two kinds of evidence we have been examining, but it is grounded in two aspects of that-which-regions. Medita-tive thinking as an openness and opening may be said to be grounded in that-which-regions as undisclosed, as veiled. And meditative thinking as involving the resolve for truth may be said to be grounded in that-which-regions as dis-

---

20. Cf. *Identität und Differenz*, p. 51.
21. "Conversation," p. 85 below. My italics.

closed, as unveiled. Yet as soon as we state the relation of meditative thinking to its grounds in this way, we suggest strongly that these grounds are related, since "that-which-regions and its nature can't really be two different things . . . the self of that-which-regions is presumably its nature and identical with itself."[22] And implicit in this suggestion (which, indeed, Heidegger holds to be correct) is a further insight. If we could understand the relation of the two aspects of meditative thinking, this would give us the clue to the sense in which that-which-regions and its nature are related and together ground meditative thinking as a whole and so man.

Perhaps the relation of the two aspects of meditative thinking which we have kept apart here is not too difficult to sketch. Heidegger very early in the Conversation formulates what he calls a "daring definition" of thinking. "Then thinking would be coming-into-the-nearness of distance."[23] The movement of thinking referred to here is just the turning of thought toward what is given, just the opening of thought to the given as such; *and* the approaching of what is given through the demand in thought that this be articulated and so become true. We may conceive of the turning toward the given and the opening to the given as setting the given at a distance, for this movement distinguishes thinking from its given content. And we may conceive of the resolve for truth as a movement of approach, as nearing the given, since this movement elicits and reveals. And if we so conceive meditative thinking in its two aspects as nearing and distancing, then, as Heidegger says, ". . .

22. "Conversation," p. 86 below.
23. "Conversation," p. 68 below.

perhaps we can express our experience during this conversation by saying that we are coming near to and so at the same time remaining distant from that-which-regions. . . ."[24] If so, this complex movement would provide the concept needed to understand the identity of that-which-regions and its nature.

Because that-which-regions regions all, gathering everything together and letting everything return to itself, to rest in its own identity. Then that-which-regions itself would be nearing and distancing . . . a characterization which should not be thought of dialectically . . . [but] in accordance with the nature of thinking. . . .[25]

This third compatibility of thinking and that-which-regions must not be viewed statically; it must be comprehended as an intricate movement weaving the given and veiled aspect of that-which-regions into its unveiled and articulated aspect. Not any part, but the whole of this movement is Being.

This bold characterization of Being has been reached through man, for Heidegger's claim to have proceeded from man to Being rests upon his analysis of meditative thinking. In this analysis there are central strands of three kinds. In the first place, there are the two analyses which claim to show that meditative thinking can be grounded in that-which-regions as such and in the *nature* of that-which-regions. We have considered these analyses in the last few pages. They are analyses that lead from certain specifiable characteristics of thinking to what grounds thinking so far as it has these characteristics. We refer to the characteristics of opening and openness on the one hand, and to the resolve for truth on the other. The third analysis support-

24. "Conversation," p. 86 below.
25. "Conversation," p. 86 below.

ing Heidegger's claim that Being is attainable has just been given. It is an analysis suggesting that the continuity between the two aspects of thought which is found in the movement of "coming-into-the-nearness of distance" must reflect a continuity between the apparently different grounds of these aspects, that is, between that-which-regions as such and its nature.

As soon as this final analysis is presented it justifies shifting perspective from man to Being. It justifies such statements as "Truth's nature can come forth independently of man only because the nature of man (as releasement to that-which-regions) is used by that-which-regions in regioning both with respect to man and to sustain determining. Evidently truth's independence *from* man is a relation *to* human nature, a relation which rests on the regioning of human nature into that-which-regions."[26] It justifies asking such a question as, "Yet what then would be the nature of thinking if that-which-regions is the nearness of distance?"[27] From the perspective afforded by this final analysis, one is able to see man's nature, the nature of thinking, as determined by Being, as ". . . the essentially human relation to that-which-regions. . . ."[28] Evidently we stand here in the midst of the ultimate, having stepped beyond our subjective human perspective—yet a word of caution is necessary! And, indeed, Heidegger cautions us in a number of ways. Thus, to depict this view he uses, and says he uses, the subjunctive mood, ". . . for some time . . . we have said everything in the mode of supposition

26. "Conversation," p. 84 below.
27. "Conversation," p. 86 below.
28. "Conversation," p. 87 below.

only."[29] Thus, to name the nature of thinking in its de-
pendence upon that-which-regions, he falls back upon the
Greek word comprising Heraclitus' 122nd Fragment, and
then deliberately reads meaning into it until it seems to be
"the best name for what we have found."[30] But at just this
point he adds, "Which in its nature, nevertheless, we are
still seeking."[31] And, finally, he personifies Being in the
imaginative figure of Night and recasts the argument
imaginatively, for "the child in man."[32]

By such cautionary words and modes of expression,
Heidegger wishes to prevent too literal and too strict an interpretation of what can be said from the midst of the ultimate. We may understand the significance of this caution
if we recall that it is the continuity, attained in the inter-
weaving in thinking of opening and openness on the one
hand, and the resolve for truth on the other, that provides
the final step to Being. We may be inclined to forget, in
the intoxicating moment when we stand on this step, that
the continuity achieved is specific and particular, that it is
just that continuity which it is, and that it probably will
vanish. If we forget this, we shall forget, too, that the
continuity of thinking as specific and particular must reflect
something specific and particular about the movement
identifying that-which-regions as such and its nature, something of the vanishing which is an aspect of Being.

JOHN M. ANDERSON

29. "Conversation," p. 85 below.
30. "Conversation," p. 89 below.
31. "Conversation," p. 89 below.
32. "Conversation," p. 89 below.

DISCOURSE ON THINKING

I

MEMORIAL ADDRESS*

Let my first public word in my home town be a word of thanks.

I thank my homeland for all that it has given me along the path of my life. I have tried to explain the nature of this endowment in those few pages entitled "Der Feldweg"[1] which first appeared in 1949 in a book honoring the hundredth anniversary of the death of Conradin Kreutzer.[2] I thank Mayor Schühle for his warm-hearted welcome. And I am especially grateful for the privilege of giving the memorial address at today's ceremony.

Honored Guests, Friends and Neighbors! We are gathered together in commemoration of the composer Conradin Kreutzer, a native of our region. If we are to honor a man whose calling it is to be creative, we must, above all, duly honor his work. In the case of a musician this is done through the performance of his compositions.

Conradin Kreutzer's compositions ring forth today in

* This speech was presented at the celebration of the 175th birthday of the composer Conradin Kreutzer on October 30, 1955, in Messkirch.
1. Country Path (Tr.).
2. Conradin Kreutzer (1780–1849), German composer and conductor. He was highly productive in concert, chamber and church music, operas and musical plays, choruses and songs. Of his works some of his choruses for men and one of his operas are still well known in Germany. (Tr.)

song and chorus, in opera and in chamber music. In these sounds the artist himself is present; for the master's presence *in the work* is the only true presence. The greater the master, the more completely his person vanishes behind his work.

The musicians and singers who take part in today's celebration are a warrant that Conradin Kreutzer's work will come to be heard on this occasion.

But does this alone constitute a memorial celebration? A memorial celebration means that we think back, that we *think*. Yet what are we to think and to say at a memorial which is devoted to a composer? Is it not the distinction of music to "speak" through the sounding of tones and so not to need ordinary language, the language of words? So they say. And yet the question remains: Do playing and singing alone make our celebration a thoughtful celebration, one in which we think? Hardly! And so a "memorial address" has been put on the program. It is to help us to think back both to the composer we honor and to his work. These memories come alive as soon as we relate the story of Conradin Kreutzer's life, and recount and describe his works. Through such a relating we can find much that is joyful and sorrowful, much that is instructive and exemplary. But at bottom we merely allow ourselves to be entertained by such a talk. In listening to such a story, no thinking at all is needed, no reflecting is demanded on what concerns each one of us immediately and continuously in his very being. Thus even a memorial address gives no assurance that we will think at a memorial celebration.

Let us not fool ourselves. All of us, including those who think professionally, as it were, are often enough thought-poor; we all are far too easily thought-less. Thoughtlessness is an uncanny visitor who comes and goes everywhere in today's world. For nowadays we take in everything in the quickest and cheapest way, only to forget it just as quickly, instantly. Thus one gathering follows on the heels of another. Commemorative celebrations grow poorer and poorer in thought. Commemoration and thoughtlessness are found side by side.

But even while we are thoughtless, we do not give up our capacity to think. We rather use this capacity implicitly, though strangely: that is, in thoughtlessness we let it lie fallow. Still only that can lie fallow which in itself is a ground for growth, such as a field. An expressway, where nothing grows, cannot be a fallow field. Just as we can grow deaf only because we hear, just as we can grow old only because we were young; so we can grow thought-poor or even thought-less only because man at the core of his being has the capacity to think; has "spirit and reason" and is destined to think. We can only lose or, as the phrase goes, get loose from that which we knowingly or unknowingly possess.

The growing thoughtlessness must, therefore, spring from some process that gnaws at the very marrow of man today: man today is in *flight from thinking*. This flight-from-thought is the ground of thoughtlessness. But part of this flight is that man will neither see nor admit it. Man today will even flatly deny this flight from thinking. He will assert the opposite. He will say—and quite rightly— that there were at no time such far-reaching plans, so many inquiries in so many areas, research carried on as passionately as today. Of course. And this display of ingenuity and deliberation has its own great usefulness. Such thought remains indispensable. But—it also remains true that it is thinking of a special kind.

Its peculiarity consists in the fact that whenever we plan, research, and organize, we always reckon with conditions that are given. We take them into account with the calculated intention of their serving specific purposes. Thus we can count on definite results. This calculation is the mark of all thinking that plans and investigates. Such thinking remains calculation even if it neither works with numbers nor uses an adding machine or computer. Calculative thinking computes. It computes ever new, ever more promising and at the same time more economical possibilities. Calculative thinking races from one prospect to the next. Calculative thinking never stops, never collects itself. Calculative thinking is not meditative thinking, not thinking which contemplates the meaning which reigns in everything that is.

There are, then, two kinds of thinking, each justified and needed in its own way: calculative thinking and meditative thinking.

This meditative thinking is what we have in mind when we say that contemporary man is in flight-from-thinking. Yet you may protest: mere meditative thinking finds itself floating unaware above reality. It loses touch. It is worthless for dealing with current business. It profits nothing in carrying out practical affairs.

And you may say, finally, that mere meditative thinking, persevering meditation, is "above" the reach of ordinary understanding. In this excuse only this much is true, meditative thinking does not just happen by itself any more than does calculative thinking. At times it requires a greater effort. It demands more practice. It is in need of even more delicate care than any other genuine craft. But it must also be able to bide its time, to await as does the farmer, whether the seed will come up and ripen.

Yet anyone can follow the path of meditative thinking in his own manner and within his own limits. Why? Because man is a *thinking*, that is, a *meditating* being. Thus meditative thinking need by no means be "high-flown." It is enough if we dwell on what lies close and meditate on what is closest; upon that which concerns us, each one of us, here and now; here, on this patch of home ground; now, in the present hour of history.

What does this celebration suggest to us, in case we are ready to meditate? Then we notice that a work of art has flowered in the ground of our homeland. As we hold this simple fact in mind, we cannot help remembering at once that during the last two centuries great poets and thinkers have been brought forth from the Swabian land. Thinking about it further makes clear at once that Central Germany is likewise such a land, and so are East Prussia, Silesia, and Bohemia.

We grow thoughtful and ask: does not the flourishing of any genuine work depend upon its roots in a native soil? Johann Peter Hebel once wrote: "We are plants which—whether we like to admit it to ourselves or not—must with our roots rise out of the earth in order to bloom in the ether and to bear fruit." (*Works*, ed. Altwegg III, 314.)

The poet means to say: For a truly joyous and salutary human work to flourish, man must be able to mount from the depth of his home ground up into the ether. Ether here means the free air of the high heavens, the open realm of the spirit.

We grow more thoughtful and ask: does this claim of Johann Peter Hebel hold today? Does man still dwell calmly between heaven and earth? Does a meditative spirit still reign over the land? Is there still a life-giving homeland in whose ground man may stand rooted, that is, be autochthonic?

Many Germans have lost their homeland, have had to leave their villages and towns, have been driven from their native soil. Countless others whose homeland was saved, have yet wandered off. They have been caught up in the turmoil of the big cities, and have resettled in the wastelands of industrial districts. They are strangers now to their former homeland. And those who *have* stayed on in their homeland? Often they are still more homeless than those who have been driven from their homeland. Hourly and daily they are chained to radio and television. Week after week the movies carry them off into uncommon, but often merely common, realms of the imagination, and give the illusion of a world that is no world. Picture magazines are everywhere available. All that with which modern techniques of communication stimulate, assail, and drive man—all that is already much closer to man today than his fields around his farmstead, closer than the sky over the earth, closer than the change from night to day, closer than the conventions and customs of his village, than the tradition of his native world.

We grow more thoughtful and ask: What is happening here—with those driven from their homeland no less than with those who have remained? Answer: the *rootedness*,

the *autochthony*, of man is threatened today at its core![3]
Even more: The loss of rootedness is caused not merely by
circumstance and fortune, nor does it stem only from the
negligence and the superficiality of man's way of life.
The loss of autochthony springs from the spirit of the age
into which all of us were born.

We grow still more thoughtful and ask: If this is so, can
man, can man's work in the future still be expected to thrive
in the fertile ground of a homeland and mount into the
ether, into the far reaches of the heavens and the spirit?
Or will everything now fall into the clutches of planning
and calculation, of organization and automation?

If we reflect upon what our celebration today suggests,
then we must observe the loss of man's autochthony with
which our age is threatened. And we ask: What really is
happening in our age? By what is it characterized?

The age that is now beginning has been called of late
the atomic age. Its most conspicuous symbol is the atom
bomb. But this symbolizes only the obvious; for it was
recognized at once that atomic energy can be used also for
peaceful purposes. Nuclear physicists everywhere are busy
with vast plans to implement the peaceful uses of atomic
energy. The great industrial corporations of the leading
countries, first of all England, have figured out already that
atomic energy can develop into a gigantic business.
Through this atomic business a new era of happiness is en-
visioned. Nuclear science, too, does not stand idly by. It
publicly proclaims this era of happiness. Thus in July of
this year at Lake Constance, eighteen Nobel Prize winners

3. The German *Bodenständigkeit* is translated *rootedness* or *autochthony*
depending on a literal or a more figurative connotation. (Tr.)

stated in a proclamation: "Science [and that is modern natural science] is a road to a happier human life."

What is the sense of this statement? Does it spring from reflection? Does it ever ponder on the meaning of the atomic age? No! For if we rest content with this statement of science, we remain as far as possible from a reflective insight into our age. Why? Because we forget to ponder. Because we forget to ask: What is the ground that enabled modern technology to discover and set free new energies in nature?

This is due to a revolution in leading concepts which has been going on for the past several centuries, and by which man is placed in a different world. This radical revolution in outlook has come about in modern philosophy. From this arises a completely new relation of man to the world and his place in it. The world now appears as an object open to the attacks of calculative thought, attacks that nothing is believed able any longer to resist. Nature becomes a gigantic gasoline station, an energy source for modern technology and industry. This relation of man to the world as such, in principle a technical one, developed in the seventeenth century first and only in Europe. It long remained unknown in other continents, and it was altogether alien to former ages and histories.

The power concealed in modern technology determines the relation of man to that which exists. It rules the whole earth. Indeed, already man is beginning to advance beyond the earth into outer space. In not quite twenty years, such gigantic sources of power have become known through the discovery of atomic energy that in the foreseeable future the world's demands for energy of any kind will be ensured forever. Soon the procurement of the new energies will no longer be tied to certain countries and continents, as is the occurrence of coal, oil, and timber. In the foreseeable future it will be possible to build atomic power stations anywhere on earth.

Thus the decisive question of science and technology to-day is no longer: Where do we find sufficient quantities of fuel? The decisive question now runs: In what way can we tame and direct the unimaginably vast amounts of atomic energies, and so secure mankind against the danger that these gigantic energies suddenly—even without mili-tary actions—break out somewhere, "run away" and de-stroy everything?

If the taming of atomic energy is successful, and it will be successful, then a totally new era of technical develop-ment will begin. What we know now as the technology of film and television, of transportation and especially air transportation, of news reporting, and as medical and nutritional technology, is presumably only a crude start. No one can foresee the radical changes to come. But tech-nological advance will move faster and faster and can never be stopped. In all areas of his existence, man will be en-circled ever more tightly by the forces of technology. These forces, which everywhere and every minute claim, enchain, drag along, press and impose upon man under the form of some technical contrivance or other—these forces, since man has not made them, have moved long since beyond his will and have outgrown his capacity for decision.

But this too is characteristic of the new world of technol-ogy, that its accomplishments come most speedily to be known and publicly admired. Thus today everyone will be able to read what this talk says about technology in any competently managed picture magazine or hear it on the radio. But—it is one thing to have heard and read something, that is, merely to take notice; it is another thing to understand what we have heard and read, that is, to ponder.

The international meeting of Nobel Prize winners took place again in the summer of this year of 1955 in Lindau. There the American chemist, Stanley, had this to say: "The hour is near when life will be placed in the hands of the chemist who will be able to synthesize, split and change living substance at will." We take notice of such a statement. We even marvel at the daring of scientific research, without thinking about it. We do not stop to consider that an attack with technological means is being prepared upon the life and nature of man compared with which the explosion of the hydrogen bomb means little. For precisely if the hydrogen bombs do *not* explode and human life on earth is preserved, an uncanny change in the world moves upon us.

Yet it is not that the world is becoming entirely technical which is really uncanny. Far more uncanny is our being unprepared for this transformation, our inability to confront meditatively what is really dawning in this age.

No single man, no group of men, no commission of prominent statesmen, scientists, and technicians, no conference of leaders of commerce and industry, can brake or direct the progress of history in the atomic age. No merely human organization is capable of gaining dominion over it.

Is man, then, a defenseless and perplexed victim at the

mercy of the irresistible superior power of technology? He would be if man today abandons any intention to pit meditative thinking decisively against merely calculative thinking. But once meditative thinking awakens, it must be at work unceasingly and on every last occasion—hence, also, here and now at this commemoration. For here we are considering what is threatened especially in the atomic age: the autochthony of the works of man.

Thus we ask now: even if the old rootedness is being lost in this age, may not a new ground and foundation be granted again to man, a foundation and ground out of which man's nature and all his works can flourish in a new way even in the atomic age?

What could the ground and foundation be for the new autochthony? Perhaps the answer we are looking for lies at hand; so near that we all too easily overlook it. For the way to what is near is always the longest and thus the hardest for us humans. This way is the way of meditative thinking. Meditative thinking demands of us not to cling one-sidedly to a single idea, nor to run down a one-track course of ideas. Meditative thinking demands of us that we engage ourselves with what at first sight does not go together at all.

Let us give it a trial. For all of us, the arrangements, devices, and machinery of technology are to a greater or lesser extent indispensable. It would be foolish to attack technology blindly. It would be shortsighted to condemn it as the work of the devil. We depend on technical devices; they even challenge us to ever greater advances. But suddenly and unaware we find ourselves so firmly shackled to these technical devices that we fall into bondage to them.

Still we can act otherwise. We can use technical devices, and yet with proper use also keep ourselves so free of them, that we may let go of them any time. We can use technical devices as they ought to be used, and also let them alone as something which does not affect our inner and real core. We can affirm the unavoidable use of technical devices, and also deny them the right to dominate us, and so to warp, confuse, and lay waste our nature.

But will not saying both yes and no this way to technical devices make our relation to technology ambivalent and insecure? On the contrary! Our relation to technology will become wonderfully simple and relaxed. We let technical devices enter our daily life, and at the same time leave them outside, that is, let them alone, as things which are nothing absolute but remain dependent upon something higher. I would call this comportment toward technology which expresses "yes" and at the same time "no," by an old word, *releasement toward things*.[4]

Having this comportment we no longer view things only in a technical way. It gives us clear vision and we notice that while the production and use of machines demands of us another relation to things, it is not a meaningless relation. Farming and agriculture, for example, now have turned into a motorized food industry. Thus here, evidently, as

4. *Die Gelassenheit zu den Dingen. Gelassenheit,* although used today in German in the sense of "composure," "calmness," and "unconcern," also has older meanings, being used by early German mystics (as Meister Eckhart) in the sense of letting the world go and giving oneself to God. "Releasement" is not as old a word in English, but because it is rare and so free from too specific connotative meanings, it can carry with relative ease the very special and complex meanings which are implicit here and made explicit in the Conversation which follows. (Tr.)

elsewhere, a profound change is taking place in man's relation to nature and to the world. But the meaning that reigns
in this change remains obscure.

There is then in all technical processes a meaning,
not invented or made by us, which lays claim to what
man does and leaves undone. We do not know the significance of the uncanny increasing dominance of atomic
technology. *The meaning pervading technology hides itself.* But if we explicitly and continuously heed the fact that
such hidden meaning touches us everywhere in the world
of technology, we stand at once within the realm of that
which hides itself from us, and hides itself just in approaching us. That which shows itself and at the same
time withdraws is the essential trait of what we call the
mystery. I call the comportment which enables us to keep
open to the meaning hidden in technology, *openness to the
mystery*.

Releasement toward things and openness to the mystery
belong together. They grant us the possibility of dwelling
in the world in a totally different way. They promise us a
new ground and foundation upon which we can stand and
endure in the world of technology without being imperiled
by it.

Releasement toward things and openness to the mystery
give us a vision of a new autochthony which someday even
might be fit to recapture the old and now rapidly disappear-
ing autochthony in a changed form.

But for the time being—we do not know for how long—
man finds himself in a perilous situation. Why? Just because a third world war might break out unexpectedly and
bring about the complete annihilation of humanity and the

destruction of the earth? No. In this dawning atomic age a far greater danger threatens—precisely when the danger of a third world war has been removed. A strange assertion! Strange indeed, but only as long as we do not meditate.

In what sense is the statement just made valid? This assertion is valid in the sense that the approaching tide of technological revolution in the atomic age could so captivate, bewitch, dazzle, and beguile man that calculative thinking may someday come to be accepted and practiced *as the only* way of thinking.

What great danger then might move upon us? Then there might go hand in hand with the greatest ingenuity in calculative planning and inventing indifference toward meditative thinking, total thoughtlessness. And then? Then man would have denied and thrown away his own special nature—that he is a meditative being. Therefore, the issue is the saving of man's essential nature. Therefore, the issue is keeping meditative thinking alive.

Yet releasement toward things and openness to the mystery never happen of themselves. They do not befall us accidentally. Both flourish only through persistent, courageous thinking.

Perhaps today's memorial celebration will prompt us toward this. If we respond to the prompting, we think of Conradin Kreutzer by thinking of the origin of his work, the life-giving powers of his Heuberg homeland. And it is *we* who *think* if we know ourselves here and now as the men who must find and prepare the way into the atomic age, through it and out of it.

If releasement toward things and openness to the mystery awaken within us, then we should arrive at a path that will lead to a new ground and foundation. In that ground the creativity which produces lasting works could strike new roots.

Thus in a different manner and in a changed age, the truth of what Johann Peter Hebel says should be renewed:

We are plants which—whether we like to admit it to ourselves or not—must with our roots rise out of the earth in order to bloom in the ether and to bear fruit.

II

CONVERSATION ON
A COUNTRY PATH
ABOUT THINKING*

Scientist: Toward the last you stated that the question concerning man's nature is not a question about man.

Teacher: I said only that the question concerning man's nature makes a consideration whether this is the case unavoidable.

Scientist: Even so, it is a mystery to me how man's nature is ever to be found by looking away from man.

Teacher: It is a mystery to me too; so I seek to clarify how far this is possible, or perhaps even necessary.—

Scientist: To behold man's nature without looking at man!

Teacher: Why not? If thinking is what distinguishes man's nature, then surely the essence of this nature, namely the nature of thinking, can be seen only by looking away from thinking.

Scholar: But thinking, understood in the traditional way, as re-presenting is a kind of willing; Kant, too, under-

---

* This discourse was taken from a conversation written down in 1944–45 between a scientist, a scholar, and a teacher.

stands thinking this way when he characterizes it as spontaneity. To think is to will, and to will is to think.

Scientist: Then the statement that the nature of thinking is something other than thinking means that thinking is something other than willing.

Teacher: And that is why, in answer to your question as to what I really wanted from our meditation on the nature of thinking, I replied: I want non-willing.

Scientist: Meanwhile this formulation has proved ambiguous.

Scholar: Non-willing, for one thing, means a willing in such a way as to involve negation, be it even in the sense of a negation which is directed at willing and renounces it. Non-willing means, therefore: willingly to renounce willing. And the term non-willing means, further, what remains absolutely outside any kind of will.

Scientist: So that it can never be carried out or reached by any willing.

Teacher: But perhaps we come nearer to it by a willing in the first sense of non-willing.

Scholar: You see, then, the two senses of non-willing as standing in a definite relation to each other.

Teacher: Not only do I see this relation, I confess that ever since I have tried to reflect on what moves our conversation, it has claimed my attention, if not challenged me.

Scientist: Am I right if I state the relation of the one sense of non-willing to the other as follows? You want a non-willing in the sense of a renouncing of willing, so that through this we may release, or at least prepare to release, ourselves to the sought-for essence of a thinking that is not a willing.

Teacher: You are not only right, but by the gods! as I would say if they had not flown from us, you have uncovered something essential.

Scholar: I should now be tempted to say that you, in your interpretation of the ambiguous talk about non-willing, have surpassed both us and yourself—if anyone were entitled to mete out praise and if that were not contrary to the style of our conversations.

Scientist: That I succeeded in this, was not my doing but that of the night having set in, which without forcing compels concentration.

Scholar: It leaves us time for meditating by slowing down our pace.

Teacher: That is why we are still far from human habitation.

Scientist: Ever more openly I am coming to trust in the inconspicuous guide who takes us by the hand—or better said, by the word—in this conversation.

Scholar: We need this guidance, because our conversation becomes ever more difficult.

Teacher: If by "difficult" you mean the unaccustomed task which consists in weaning ourselves from will.

Scholar: Will, you say, and not merely willing . . .

Scientist: . . . and so, you state an exciting demand in a released manner.

Teacher: If only I possessed already the right releasement, then I would soon be freed of that task of weaning.

Scholar: So far as we can wean ourselves from willing, we contribute to the awakening of releasement.

Teacher: Say rather, to keeping awake for releasement.

Scholar: Why not, to the awakening?

Teacher: Because on our own we do not awaken release-ment in ourselves.

Scientist: Thus releasement is effected from somewhere else.

Teacher: Not effected, but let in.

Scholar: To be sure I don't know yet what the word release-ment means; but I seem to presage that releasement awakens when our nature is let-in so as to have dealings with that which is not a willing.

Scientist: You speak without letup of a letting-be and give the impression that what is meant is a kind of passivity. All the same, I think I understand that it is in no way a matter of weakly allowing things to slide and drift along.

Scholar: Perhaps a higher acting is concealed in release-ment than is found in all the actions within the world and in the machinations of all mankind . . .

Teacher: . . . which higher acting is yet no activity.

Scientist: Then releasement lies—if we may use the word lie—beyond the distinction between activity and pas-sivity . . .

Scholar: . . . because releasement does *not* belong to the domain of the will.

Scientist: The transition from willing into releasement is what seems difficult to me.

Teacher: And all the more, since the nature of release-ment is still hidden.

Scholar: Especially so because even releasement can still be thought of as within the domain of will, as is the case with old masters of thought such as Meister Eckhart.

Teacher: From whom, all the same, much can be learned.

Scholar: Certainly; but what we have called releasement evidently does not mean casting off sinful selfishness and letting self-will go in favor of the divine will.

Teacher: No, not that.

Scientist: In many respects it is clear to me what the word releasement should not signify for us. But at the same time, I know less and less what we are talking about. We are trying to determine the nature of thinking. What has releasement to do with thinking?

Teacher: Nothing if we conceive thinking in the traditional way as re-presenting. Yet perhaps the nature of thinking we are seeking is fixed in releasement.

Scientist: With the best of will, I can not re-present to myself this nature of thinking.

Teacher: Precisely because this will of yours and your mode of thinking as re-presenting prevent it.

Scientist: But then, what in the world am I to do?

Scholar: I am asking myself that too.

Teacher: We are to do nothing but wait.

Scholar: That is poor consolation.

Teacher: Poor or not, we should not await consolation—something we would still be doing if we became disconsolate.

Scientist: Then what are we to wait for? And where are we to wait? I hardly know anymore who and where I am.

Teacher: None of us knows that, as soon as we stop fooling ourselves.

Scholar: And yet we still have our path?

Teacher: To be sure. But by forgetting it too quickly we give up thinking.

Scientist: What are we still to think about, in order to pass over to and into the nature of thinking which we have not yet come to know?

Teacher: Why, about that from whence alone such a transition can happen.

Scholar: That means that you would not discard the traditional view of the nature of thinking?

Teacher: Have you forgotten what I said in our earlier conversation about what is revolutionary?

Scientist: Forgetfulness does seem to be an especial danger in such conversations.

Scholar: So now, if I understand correctly, we are to view what we call releasement in connection with the nature of thinking as talked about, even though we hardly know it and above all are unable to place it properly.

Teacher: I mean exactly that.

Scientist: Previously, we had come to see thinking in the form of transcendental-horizonal re-presenting.

Scholar: This re-presenting, for instance, places before us what is typical of a tree, of a pitcher, of a bowl, of a stone, of plants, and of animals as that view into which we look when one thing confronts us in the appearance of a tree, another thing in the appearance of a pitcher, this in the appearance of a bowl, various things in the appearance of stones, many in the appearance of plants, and many in the appearance of animals.

Scientist: You describe, once again, the horizon which encircles the view of a thing—the field of vision.

Teacher: It goes beyond the appearance of the objects.

Scholar: Just as transcendence passes beyond the perception of objects.

Teacher: Thus we determine what is called horizon and transcendence by means of this going beyond and passing beyond . . .

Scholar: . . . which refer back to objects and our representing of objects.

Teacher: Horizon and transcendence, thus, are experienced and determined only relative to objects and our representing them.

Scholar: Why do you stress this?

Teacher: To suggest that in this way what lets the horizon be what it is has not yet been encountered at all.

Scientist: What do you have in mind in this statement?

Teacher: We say that we look into the horizon. Therefore the field of vision is something open, but its openness is not due to our looking.

Scholar: Likewise we do not place the appearance of objects, which the view within a field of vision offers us, into this openness . . .

Scientist: . . . rather that comes out of this to meet us.

Teacher: What is evident of the horizon, then, is but the side facing us of an openness which surrounds us; an openness which is filled with views of the appearances of what to our re-presenting are objects.

Scientist: In consequence the horizon is still something else besides a horizon. Yet after what has been said this something else is the other side of itself, and so the same as itself. You say that the horizon is the openness which surrounds us. But what is this openness as such, if we disregard that it can also appear as the horizon of our re-presenting?

Teacher: It strikes me as something like a *region,* an enchanted region where everything belonging there returns to that in which it rests.

Scholar: I'm not sure I understand what you say now.

Teacher: I don't understand it either, if by "understanding" you mean the capacity to re-present what is put before us as if sheltered amid the familiar and so secured; for I, too, lack the familiar in which to place what I tried to say about openness as a region.

Scientist: That is perhaps impossible here, if for no other reason than because presumably what you call a region is exactly that which alone permits all sheltering.

Teacher: I mean something like this; but not only this.

Scholar: You spoke of "a" region in which everything returns to itself. Strictly speaking, a region for everything is not one region among many, but the region of all regions.

Teacher: You are right; what is in question is *the* region.

Scientist: And the enchantment of this region might well be the reign of its nature, its regioning, if I may call it that.

Scholar: It seems a region holds what comes forward to meet us; but we also said of the horizon that out of the view which it encircles, the appearance of objects comes to meet us. If now we comprehend the horizon through the region, we take the region itself as that which comes to meet us.

Teacher: In this way, indeed, we would characterize the region through its relation to us, just as we did a moment ago with the horizon—whereas we are searching for the nature, in itself, of the openness that surrounds us. If we now say this is the region, and say it with the meaning we just gave it, then the word must name something else.

Scientist: Moreover, the coming to meet us is not at all a basic characteristic of region, let alone the basic characteristic. What does this word imply?

Scholar: In its older form it is *"Gegnet"* and means open expanse. Can anything be learned from this about the nature of what we now call the region?

Teacher: The region gathers, just as if nothing were happening, each to each and each to all into an abiding, while resting in itself. Regioning is a gathering and re-sheltering for an expanded resting in an abiding.

Scholar: So the region itself is at once an expanse and an abiding. It abides into the expanse of resting. It expands into the abiding of what has freely turned toward itself. In view of this usage of the word, we may also say "that-which-regions" in place of the familiar "region."[1]

Teacher: That-which-regions is an abiding expanse which, gathering all, opens itself, so that in it openness is halted and held, letting everything merge in its own resting.

Scientist: I believe I see that-which-regions as withdrawing rather than coming to meet us . . .

1. The German word for region is *Gegend*. What is in question here, however, is not region in general, but as Heidegger says, "the region of all regions" (*"die Gegend aller Gegenden"*) or *the* region. Heidegger uses an old variant of *Gegend* as the word for *the* region: *die Gegnet*— a word that still occurs in spoken German although only in South German dialects. Since an analogous variant is not available for the English counterpart, *die Gegnet* has been rendered in the text by the phrase *that-which-regions*. *That-which-regions* reflects a movement attributed by Heidegger to *die Gegnet* and further emphasized by his use of the verb *gegnen* (to region). (Tr.)

Scholar: . . . so that things which appear in that-which-regions no longer have the character of objects.

Teacher: They not only no longer stand opposite us, they no longer stand at all.

Scientist: Do they lie, then, or how about them?

Teacher: They lie, if by this we mean that resting which was just discussed.

Scientist: But where do things rest? What does resting consist of?

Teacher: They rest in the return to the abiding of the expanse of their self-belonging.

Scholar: But in this return, which after all is movement, can there be rest?

Teacher: Indeed there can, if rest is the seat and the reign of all movement.

Scientist: I must confess that I can't quite re-present in my mind all that you say about region, expanse and abiding, and about return and resting.

Scholar: Probably it can't be re-presented at all, in so far as in re-presenting everything has become an object that stands opposite us within a horizon.

Scientist: Then we can't really describe what we have named?

Teacher: No. Any description would reify it.

Scholar: Neverthless it lets itself be named, and being named it can be thought about . . .

Teacher: . . . only if thinking is no longer re-presenting.

Scientist: But then what else should it be?

Teacher: Perhaps we now are close to being released into the nature of thinking . . .

Scholar: . . . through waiting for its nature.

Teacher: Waiting, all right; but never awaiting, for awaiting already links itself with re-presenting and what is re-presented.

Scholar: Waiting, however, lets go of that; or rather I should say that waiting lets re-presenting entirely alone. It really has no object.

Scientist: Yet if we wait we always wait for something.

Scholar: Certainly, but as soon as we re-present to ourselves and fix upon that for which we wait, we really wait no longer.

Teacher: In waiting we leave open what we are waiting for.

Scholar: Why?

Teacher: Because waiting releases itself into openness . . .

Scholar: . . . into the expanse of distance . . .

Teacher: . . . in whose nearness it finds the abiding in which it remains.

Scientist: But remaining is a returning.

Scholar: Openness itself would be that for which we could do nothing but wait.

Scientist: But openness itself is that-which-regions . . .

Teacher: . . . into which we are released by way of waiting, when we think.

Scientist: Then thinking would be coming-into-the-nearness of distance.

Scholar: That is a daring definition of its nature, which we have chanced upon.

Scientist: I only brought together that which we have named, but without re-presenting anything to myself.

Teacher: Yet you have thought something.

Scientist: Or, really, waited for something without knowing for what.

Scholar: But how come you suddenly could wait?

Scientist: As I see more clearly just now, all during our conversation I have been waiting for the arrival of the nature of thinking. But waiting itself has become clearer to me now and therewith this too, that presumably we all became more waitful along our path.

Teacher: Can you tell us how this is so?

Scientist: I'll be glad to try, providing I don't have to run the risk that you will at once pin me down to particular words.

Teacher: In our conversations, we don't usually do that.

Scholar: Rather, we see to it that we move freely in the realm of words.

Teacher: Because a word does not and never can re-present anything; but signifies something, that is, shows something as abiding into the range of its expressibility.

Scientist: I am to say why I came to wait and the way I succeeded in clarifying the nature of thinking. I tried to release myself of all re-presenting, because waiting moves into openness without re-presenting anything. And, released from re-presenting, I tried to release myself purely to that-which-regions because that-which-regions is the opening of openness.

Teacher: If I have it rightly, then, you tried to let yourself into releasement.

Scientist: To be honest, I did not think of this particularly, although we just spoke of releasement. The occasion which led me to let myself into waiting in the way mentioned was more the course of the conversation than the re-presentation of the specific objects we spoke about.

Scholar: We can hardly come to releasement more fittingly than through an occasion of letting ourselves in.

Teacher: Above all when the occasion is as inconspicuous as the silent course of a conversation that moves us.

Scholar: But that means, the conversation brings us to that path which seems nothing else than releasement itself . . .

Teacher: . . . which is something like rest.

Scholar: At this point, how movement comes from rest and remains let into rest suddenly becomes clearer to me.

Teacher: Then releasement would be not only a path but a movement.

Scholar: Where does this strange path go? Where does the movement proper to it rest?

Teacher: Where else but in that-which-regions, in relation to which releasement is what it is.

Scientist: Finally I must now go back and ask, how far is it really releasement into which I tried to let myself?

Scholar: This question causes us great embarrassment.

Teacher: In which we have found ourselves constantly along our path.

Scientist: How so?

Teacher: Because what we have designated by a word never has that word hanging on it like a name plate.

Scientist: Whatever we designate has been nameless before; this is true as well of what we name releasement. What do we go by, then, in order to estimate whether and how far the name is adequate?

Scholar: Or does all designation remain an arbitrary act with regard to the nameless?

Teacher: But is it really settled that there is the nameless at all? There is much which we often cannot say, but only because the name it has does not occur to us.

Scholar: By virtue of what kind of designation would it have its name?

Teacher: Perhaps these names are not the result of designation. They are owed to a naming in which the namable, the name and the named occur altogether.

Scientist: What you just said about naming is unclear to me.

Scholar: Probably that is connected with the nature of words.

Scientist: However, what you noted about designation, and about the fact that there is nothing nameless, is clearer to me.

Scholar: Because we can test it in the case of the name releasement.

Teacher: Or have tested it already.

Scientist: How so?

Teacher: What is it that you designated by the name releasement?

Scientist: If I may say so, not I but you have used this name.

Teacher: I, as little as you, have done the designating.

Scholar: Then who did it? None of us?

Teacher: Presumably, for in the region in which we stay everything is in the best order only if it has been no one's doing.

Scientist: A mysterious region where there is nothing for which to be answerable.

Teacher: Because it is the region of the word, which is answerable to itself alone.

Scholar: For us it remains only to listen to the answer proper to the word.

Teacher: That is enough; even when our telling is only a retelling of the answer heard . . .

Scientist: . . . and when it doesn't matter in this if there is a first retelling or who does it; all the more since one often doesn't know whose tale he retells.

Scholar: So let's not quarrel over who first introduced the name, releasement, let us consider only what it is we name by it.

Scientist: And that is waiting, as the experience I referred to indicates.

Teacher: And so not something nameless, but what is already designated. What is this waiting?

Scientist: Insofar as waiting relates to openness and openness is that-which-regions, we can say that waiting is a relation to that-which-regions.

Teacher: Perhaps it is even *the* relation to that-which-regions, insofar as waiting releases itself to that-which-regions, and in doing so lets that-which-regions reign purely as such.

Scholar: Then a relation to something would be the true relation if it were held in its own nature by that to which it relates.

Teacher: The relation to that-which-regions is waiting. And waiting means: to release oneself into the openness of that-which-regions.

Scholar: Thus to go into that-which-regions.

Scientist: That sounds as if before then we had been outside that-which-regions.

Teacher: That we were, and yet we were not. Insofar as we as thinking beings (that is, beings who at the same time re-present transcendentally) stay within the horizon of transcendence, we are not and never could be outside that-which-regions. Yet the horizon is but the

side of that-which-regions turned toward our re-presenting. That-which-regions surrounds us and reveals itself
to us as the horizon.

Scholar: It seems to me that as the horizon it rather conceals itself.

Teacher: Certainly, nevertheless we are in that-which-
regions when, re-presenting transcendentally, we step
out into the horizon. And yet again we are still not in it,
so far as we have not released ourselves for that-which-
regions, as such.

Scientist: Something which happens in waiting.

Teacher: As you have said, in waiting we are released from
our transcendental relation to the horizon.

Scientist: This being-released-from is the first aspect of releasement; yet that does not hit its nature exactly, let
alone exhaust it.

Scholar: How not?

Teacher: So far as authentic releasement may come about
without necessarily being preceded by such being-released-from horizontal transcendence.

Scholar: If authentic releasement is to be the proper relation to that-which-regions, and if this relation is determined solely by what it is related to, then authentic
releasement must be based upon that-which-regions, and
must have received from it movement toward it.

Teacher: Releasement comes out of that-which-regions because in releasement man stays released to that-which-
regions and, indeed, through this itself. He is released to
it in his being, insofar as he originally belongs to it. He
belongs to it insofar as he is *appropriated* initially to that-
which-regions and, indeed, through this itself.

Scholar: In fact (supposing that it is waiting which is essential, that is, all-decisive), waiting upon something is based on our belonging in that upon which we wait.[2]

Teacher: Out of the experience of and in relation to just such waiting upon the opening of that-which-regions, waiting came to be spoken of as releasement.

Scholar: Thus waiting upon that-which-regions is named adequately.

Scientist: But if heretofore the reigning essence of thinking has been that transcendental-horizonal re-presenting from which releasement, because of its belonging to that-which-regions, releases itself; then thinking changes in releasement from such a re-presenting to waiting upon that-which-regions.

Teacher: Yet the nature of this waiting is releasement to that-which-regions. But because it is that-which-regions which then lets releasement belong to it, since resting in it, the nature of thinking lies, if I may say so, in the regioning of releasement by that-which-regions.

Scholar: Thinking is releasement to that-which-regions because its nature lies in the regioning of releasement.

Teacher: But by this you say that the nature of thinking is not determined through thinking and so not through waiting as such, but through the other-than-itself, that is, through that-which-regions which as regioning first brings forth this nature.

Scientist: I can follow, after a fashion, all that we have said now about releasement, that-which-regions, and regioning; all the same I can re-present nothing of it to myself.

2. See Introduction for comment on the use of "waiting upon," p. 23. (Tr.)

Scholar: You aren't supposed to—if you think what was said in accordance with its nature.

Scientist: You mean that we wait upon it in accordance with the changed nature of thinking.

Scholar: That is, wait upon the regioning of that-which-regions, so that this releases our nature into that-which-regions, and so into belonging to it.

Teacher: But if we are already appropriated to that-which-regions?

Scientist: What good does that do us if we aren't truly appropriated?

Scholar: Thus we are and we are not.

Scientist: Again this restless to and fro between yes and no.

Scholar: We are suspended as it were between the two.

Teacher: Yet our stand in this betweenness is waiting.

Scholar: That is the nature of releasement into which the regioning of that-which-regions regions man. We presage the nature of thinking as releasement.

Teacher: Only to forget releasement again as quickly.

Scientist: That, which I myself have experienced as waiting.

Teacher: We are to bear in mind that thinking is in no way self-subsisting releasement. Releasement to that-which-regions is thinking only as the regioning of releasement, a regioning which releases releasement into that-which-regions.

Scholar: However, that-which-regions also makes things endure in the abiding expanse. What are we to call the regioning of that-which-regions with respect to things?

Scientist: It can't be regioning with respect to man for that is the relation of that-which-regions to releasement, and releasement is said to shelter in itself the nature of thinking, whereas things themselves do not think.

Teacher: Evidently things are things through the regioning of that-which-regions as an earlier conversation on the abiding of the pitcher in the expanse of that-which-regions showed. However, the regioning of that-which-regions does not cause and effect things, as little indeed as that-which-regions effects releasement. That-which-regions in its regioning is neither the horizon of releasement; nor is it the horizon of things, whether we experience them only as objects or take them as "things-in-themselves" and in addition to objects.

Scholar: What you now say seems to me so decisive that I would like to try fixing it in scholarly terminology. Of course I know that such terminology not only freezes thought, but at the same time also renders it ambiguous with just that ambiguity which unavoidably adheres to ordinary terminology.

Teacher: After that scholarly reservation, you shouldn't hesitate to speak in a scholarly manner.

Scholar: As you state it, the relation of that-which-regions to releasement is neither a connection of cause to effect, nor the transcendental-horizonal relation. To state it still more briefly and more generally: the relation between that-which-regions and releasement, if it can still be considered a relation, can be thought of neither as ontic nor as ontological . . .

Teacher: . . . but only as regioning.

Scientist: Similarly, also, the relation between that-which-regions and the thing is neither a connection of cause to effect, nor the transcendental-horizonal relation; and hence neither an ontic nor an ontological relation.

Scholar: But evidently, the relation of that-which-regions to the thing also is not regioning with respect to man's nature.

Teacher: What are we then to call the relation of that-which-regions to the thing, if that-which-regions lets the thing abide in itself?

Scientist: It determines the thing, as thing.

Scholar: Therefore, it is best called the determining.

Scientist: But determining is not making and effecting; nor is it rendering possible in the sense of the transcendental . . .

Teacher: . . . but only the determining.

Scientist: We must first learn to think what determining is . . .

Teacher: . . . by learning to become aware of the nature of thinking . . .

Scholar: . . . that is by waiting upon determining and regioning with respect to man.

Scientist: Nevertheless, such naming is also of some help even now in bringing a certain clarity into this variety of relations. Still, precisely that relation remains undefined whose characterization concerns me most of all. I mean the relation of man to the thing.

Scholar: Why are you so persistent about this relation?

Scientist: Earlier we began by illuminating the relation between the ego and the object by way of the factual relation of thought in the physical sciences to nature. The relation between the ego and the object, the often mentioned subject-object relation, which I took to be most general, is apparently only an historical variation of the relation of man to the thing, so far as things can become objects . . .

Teacher: . . . even have become objects before they attained their nature as things.

Scholar: The same is true of the corresponding historical change of the human being to an ego . . .

Teacher: . . . which likewise emerged before the nature of man could return to itself . . .

Scientist: . . . providing we do not regard the coining of man into the *animal rationale* as final . . .

Scholar: . . . which would hardly be possible after today's conversation.

Scientist: I hesitate to decide upon this so quickly. However, something else has become clear to me. In the relation between ego and object there is concealed something historical, something which belongs to the history of man's nature.

Teacher: Only so far as man's *nature* does *not* receive its stamp from man, but from what we call that-which-regions and its regioning, does the history you presage become the history of that-which-regions.

Scientist: I can't follow you that far yet. I am content if some obscurity in the relation between ego and object is removed for me by this insight into its historical character. For when I decided in favor of the methodological type of analysis in the physical sciences, you said that this way of looking at it was historical.

Scholar: You strongly objected to that statement.

Scientist: Now I see what was meant. The program of mathematics and the experiment are grounded in the relation of man as ego to the thing as object.

Teacher: They even constitute this relation in part and unfold its historical character.

Scientist: If any examination which focuses on what is a part of history is called historical, then the methodological analysis in physics is, indeed, historical.

Scholar: Here the concept of the historical signifies a mode of knowing and is understood broadly.

Teacher: Understood, presumably, as focused upon a history which does not consist in the happenings and deeds of the world.

Scholar: Nor in the cultural achievements of man.

Scientist: But in what else?

Teacher: The historical rests in that-which-regions, and in what occurs as that-which-regions. It rests in what, coming to pass in man, regions him into his nature.

Scholar: A nature we have hardly experienced as yet, supposing it has not yet been realized in the rationality of the animal.

Scientist: In such a situation we can do nothing but wait for man's nature.

Teacher: Wait in a releasement through which we belong to that-which-regions, which still conceals its own nature.

Scholar: We presage releasement to that-which-regions as the sought-for nature of thinking.

Teacher: When we let ourselves into releasement to that-which-regions, we will non-willing.

Scientist: Releasement is indeed the release of oneself from transcendental re-presentation and so a relinquishing of the willing of a horizon. Such relinquishing no longer stems from a willing, except that the occasion for releasing oneself to belonging to that-which-regions requires a trace of willing. This trace, however, vanishes while releasing oneself and is completely extinguished in releasement.

Scholar: But in what ways is releasement related to what is not willing?

Teacher: After all we said about the enduring of the abiding expanse, about letting rest in returning, about the regioning of that-which-regions, it is hardly possible to speak of that-which-regions as will.

Scholar: Certainly the fact that on the one hand both the regioning with respect to man and the determining of that-which-regions, and on the other hand, all effecting and causing are essentially and mutually exclusive, shows how alien that is to anything pertaining to the will.

Teacher: For every will wants to actualize, and to have actuality as its element.

Scientist: Someone who heard us say this could easily get the impression that releasement floats in the realm of unreality and so in nothingness, and, lacking all power of action, is a will-less letting in of everything and, basically, the denial of the will to live!

Scholar: Do you then consider it necessary to counter this possible misunderstanding by showing in what respect something like power of action and resolve also reign in releasement?

Scientist: Yes I do, although I don't fail to recognize that all such names at once misinterpret releasement as pertaining to the will.

Scholar: So, for example, one needs to understand "re-solve" as it is understood in *Being and Time:* as the opening of man[3] *particularly* undertaken by him *for* openness . . .

Teacher: . . . which we think of as that-which-regions.

Scholar: If, in accordance with Greek story and thought, we are aware of the nature of truth as a dis-closure and recovery; then that-which-regions, we are reminded, is presumably the hidden coming forth of this nature.

Scientist: Then the nature of thinking, namely, release-ment to that-which-regions, would be a resolve for the coming forth of truth's nature.

Teacher: There could be a steadfastness hidden in release-ment, residing simply in the fact that releasement be-comes increasingly clearer about its inner nature and, being steadfast, stands within this.

Scholar: That would be behavior which did not become a swaggering comportment, but which collected itself into and remained always the composure of releasement.

Teacher: Releasement, thus composedly steadfast, would be a receiving of the regioning of that-which-regions.

Scientist: This composed steadfastness, in which the nature of releasement rests, could be said perhaps to correspond to the highest willing; but it could not. This resting in itself of releasement, which lets it belong to the region-ing of that-which-regions with respect to man . . .

Teacher: . . . and after a fashion to determining as well . . .

Scientist: . . . this steadfastness of a belonging to that-which-regions which rests in itself, still lacks a name.

Scholar: Perhaps the word "in-dwelling" could name some of this. At a friend's I once read a few lines which he

3. *Dasein* (Tr.).

had copied somewhere. They contain an explanation of this word. I still remember them. They read:

In-dwelling
Never one truth alone;
To receive intact
The coming forth of truth's nature
In return for boundless steadfastness:
Imbed the thinking heart
In the humble patience
Of unique high-minded
And noble memories.

Teacher: The in-dwelling in releasement to that-which-regions would then be the real nature of the spontaneity of thinking.

Scholar: And, following the quoted lines, thinking would be commemoration, akin to what is noble.

Teacher: In-dwelling in releasement to that-which-regions would be noble-mindedness itself.

Scientist: It seems to me that this unbelievable night entices you both to exult.

Teacher: So it does, if you mean exulting in waiting, through which we become more waitful and more void.

Scholar: Apparently emptier, but richer in contingencies.

Scientist: Then please tell me also, in your curious emptiness, in what respect releasement can be akin to what is noble.

Scholar: Noble is what has origins.

Teacher: Not only that, but abides in the origins of its nature.

Scientist: Now authentic releasement consists in this: that man in his very nature belongs to that-which-regions, i.e., he is released to it.

Scholar: Not occasionally, but—how shall we say it—prior to everything.

Scientist: The prior, of which we really can not think . . .

Teacher: . . . because the nature of thinking begins there.

Scientist: Thus man's nature is released to that-which-regions in what is prior to thought.

Scholar: Which is why we also added at once: and, indeed, through that-which-regions itself.

Teacher: It appropriates man's nature for its own regioning.

Scientist: So we have explained releasement. Nevertheless we have neglected to consider—something that struck me at once—why man's nature is appropriated by that-which-regions.

Scholar: Evidently the nature of man is released to that-which-regions because this belongs to it so essentially, that without man that-which-regions can not be a coming forth of all natures, as it is.

Scientist: This is hardly conceivable.

Teacher: It cannot be conceived at all so long as we want to re-present it to ourselves, that is, forcibly bring before ourselves an objectively given relation between an object called "man" and an object called "that-which-regions."

Scientist: That may be so. But even if we are mindful of that, doesn't there remain an insurmountable difficulty in the statement of the essential relation of human nature to that-which-regions? We have just characterized that-which-regions as the hidden nature of truth. If to be brief we say truth in place of that-which-regions, then the statement of the relation of human nature to

that-which-regions is this: human nature is given over
to truth, because truth needs man. Yet now the distin-
guishing characteristic of truth—particularly in its relation to man—is, is it not, to be what it is independent
of man?

Scholar: Here indeed you touch upon a difficulty we can
discuss only after we have explained the nature of truth
as such, and have more clearly determined the nature of
man.

Teacher: Now we are but on our way to both. Nevertheless, in order to make clearer what we have to reflect
upon if we consider this relation by itself, I would like
to paraphrase the statement about the relation of truth
to man.

Scientist: For the present, then, what you are to say about
it will be an assertion only.

Teacher: Assuredly, and I mean this: the nature of man
is released to that-which-regions and used by it accord-
ingly, for this reason alone—that man of himself has no
power over truth and it remains independent of him.
Truth's nature can come forth independently of man
only because the nature of man (as releasement to that-
which-regions) is used by that-which-regions in regioning both with respect to man and to sustain determining.
Evidently truth's independence *from* man is a relation
to human nature, a relation which rests on the regioning of human nature into that-which-regions.

Scholar: If this were so, then man, *as* in-dwelling in releasement to that-which-regions, would abide in the
origin of his nature, which in consequence we may paraphrase: man is he who is made use of for the nature of

truth. And so, abiding in his origin, man would be drawn to what is noble in his nature. He would have a presentiment of the noble mind.

Scientist: This presentiment could hardly be anything other than waiting, for the in-dwelling of releasement has been thought of as waiting.

Scholar: So if that-which-regions were the abiding expanse, patience would extend the furthest—even to the expanse of the abiding, because it can wait the longest.

Teacher: A patient noble-mindedness would be pure resting in itself of that willing, which, renouncing willing, has released itself to what is not will.

Scholar: Noble-mindedness would be the nature of thinking and thereby of thanking.

Teacher: Of that thanking which does not have to thank for something, but only thanks for being allowed to thank.

Scholar: In the nature of thinking so understood, we may have found what we seek.

Scientist: On the supposition that we have found that in which everything in our conversation appears to rest. This is the nature of that-which-regions.

Teacher: Because this is only supposed, let us add that for some time, as you have noted perhaps, we have said everything in the mode of supposition only.

Scientist: All the same I can no longer hold back the confession that while its nature has neared, that-which-regions itself seems to me to be further away than ever before.

Scholar: You mean to say that you are near to its nature and yet are distant from that-which-regions itself?

Scientist: But that-which-regions and its nature can't really be two different things—if we may speak here of things at all.

Scholar: The self of that-which-regions is presumably its nature and identical with itself.

Teacher: Then perhaps we can express our experience during this conversation by saying that we are coming near to and so at the same time remaining distant from that-which-regions; although such remaining is, to be sure, a returning.

Scholar: Only the nature of waiting and of releasement would be named in what you say.

Scientist: Then what is that nearness and distance within which that-which-regions opens up and veils itself, approaches and withdraws?

Scholar: This nearness and distance can be nothing outside that-which-regions.

Teacher: Because that-which-regions regions all, gathering everything together and letting everything return to itself, to rest in its own identity.

Scientist: Then that-which-regions itself would be nearing and distancing.

Scholar: That-which-regions itself would be the nearness of distance, and the distance of nearness . . .

Scientist: . . . a characterization which should not be thought of dialectically . . .

Teacher: . . . but how?

Scientist: In accordance with the nature of thinking so far as determined solely by that-which-regions.

Scholar: And so by waiting, by in-dwelling in releasement.

Teacher: Yet what then would be the nature of thinking if that-which-regions is the nearness of distance?

Scholar: Probably this can no longer be said in a single word. Still I know a word which up to now seemed to me appropriate to name the nature of thinking and so of knowing.

Scientist: I would like to hear this word.

Scholar: It is a word which had occurred to me as early as our first conversation. I had this in mind when I remarked at the beginning of today's conversation that I owed a valuable suggestion to our first conversation on a country path. Several times in the course of today's conversation, I was about to propose this word; but each time it seemed to fit less what neared us as the nature of thinking.

Scientist: You talk mysteriously about this thought of yours. It is as if you didn't want to reveal your discovery too soon.

Scholar: The word I have in mind was not my discovery; it is merely a scholarly thought.

Scientist: And thus, if I may say so, an historical reminder?

Scholar: If you want to put it that way. Also it would have suited well the style of today's conversation, for in the course of it we often threw in words and sentences from Greek thought. But now this word no longer suits what we are attempting to name by a single word.

Teacher: You mean the *nature of thinking* (that in-dwelling releasement to that-which-regions) which is the essentially human relation to that-which-regions, something we presage as the nearness of distance.

Scientist: Even if the word is no longer suitable, you might divulge it to us at the end of our conversation; for we again near human habitation, and in any case, must break off our discussion.

Teacher: And even if this word, earlier esteemed by you as a valuable suggestion, is no longer suitable, it could make clear to us that meanwhile we have come to confront something ineffable.

Scholar: This word is Heraclitus' word.

Scientist: From which fragment did you take it?

Scholar: This word struck me because it stands alone. It is that word, which, all by itself, constitutes Fragment 122.

Scientist: I don't know this shortest of Heraclitus' Fragments.

Scholar: It is scarcely noticed by others either, because one can do hardly anything with a single word.

Scientist: How does the fragment read?

Scholar: Ἀγχιβασίη

Scientist: What does it mean?

Scholar: The Greek word translates as "going toward."

Scientist: I regard this word as an excellent name for designating the nature of knowledge; for the character of advancing and moving toward objects is strikingly expressed in it.

Scholar: It appeared so to me too. That is also probably why it occurred to me in our first conversation, when we spoke of the action, the achievement, the work inherent in modern scientific knowledge, and, above all, in research.

Scientist: Actually, one could use this Greek word to make clear the fact that scientific research is a kind of attack on nature, but one which nevertheless allows nature to be heard. Ἀγχιβασίη; "going toward": I could think of Heraclitus' word as keyword in an essay on the nature of modern science.

Scholar: For that reason, too, I have hesitated to utter the word at this point; for it does not hit that nature of thinking which we have come to assume along our way.

Scientist: Indeed, waiting is really almost a counter-move-ment to going toward.

Scholar: Not to say a counter-rest.

Teacher: Or simply rest. Yet has it been definitely decided that 'Αγχιβασίη means going toward?

Scholar: Translated literally it says "going near."

Teacher: Perhaps we could think of it also as: "moving-into-nearness."

Scientist: You mean that quite literally in the sense of "let-ting-oneself-into-nearness"?

Teacher: About that.

Scholar: Then this word might be the name, and perhaps the best name, for what we have found.

Teacher: Which, in its nature, nevertheless, we are still seeking.

Scholar: 'Αγχιβασίη : "moving-into-nearness." The word could rather, so it seems to me now, be the name for our walk today along this country path.

Teacher: Which guided us deep into the night . . .

Scientist: . . . that gleams ever more splendidly . . .

Scholar: . . . and overwhelms the stars . . .

Teacher: . . . because it nears their distances in the heav-ens . . .

Scientist: . . . at least for the naïve observer, although not for the exact scientist.

Teacher: Ever to the child in man, night neighbors the stars.

Scholar: She binds together without seam or edge or thread.

Scientist: She neighbors; because she works only with nearness.

Scholar: If she ever works rather than rests . . .

Teacher: . . . while wondering upon the depths of the height.

Scholar: Then wonder can open what is locked?

Scientist: By way of waiting . . .

Teacher: . . . if this is released . . .

Scholar: . . . and human nature remains *appropriated* to that . . .

Teacher: . . . from whence we are called.

GLOSSARY

This glossary includes only those words especially important to the argument which are translated in more or less unusual ways.

ahnen	to presage
Ausdauer	steadfastness
Bedingnis	determining, regioning with respect to things
besinnliches Denken	meditative thinking
Beständnis	steadfastness
Boden	foundation, ground, soil
bodenständig	rooted, autochthonic
Bodenständigkeit	rootedness, autochthony
Edelmut	noble mind, noble-mindedness
eigentlich	authentic
einlassen; sich einlassen	let in, release; release oneself to, let oneself in, engage in
Entschlossenheit	resolve
Feldweg	country path
fern	distant
Ferne	distance
ge-eignet, geeignet	*appropriated*, appropriate (d)
gegnen	to region

Gegnet	that-which-regions
gelassen	released
Gelassenheit	releasement
Gelassenheit zu den Dingen	releasement toward things
Grund	ground
Grund und Boden	ground and foundation
Haltung	comportment
Herkunft	origins, origin
In-sich-beruhen	resting in itself
Inständigkeit	in-dwelling
Menschenwesen	human nature
nahe	near
Nähe	nearness
Offene, das	openness
Offenheit für das Geheimnis	openness to the mystery
rechnendes Denken	calculative thinking
Technik	technology
transzendental-horizontal	transcendental-horizonal
überlassen (adj.)	released
unheimlich	uncanny
vereignet	appropriated by
Vergegnis	regioning (with respect to man)

verhalten (adj.)	composed
Verhaltenheit	composure
verweilen	to abide, endure
verweilende Weite	abiding expanse
vorstellen	to re-present

walten	to reign
warten auf	to wait for, upon
Weile	abiding
Weile der Weite, die	abiding expanse
Weite	expanse
Weite der Weile, die	expanse of the abiding
Wesen	nature, essence (rarely)
wesende Wahrheit	coming forth of truth's nature
west, Gegnet	that-which-regions first brings forth a nature
west, Wahrheit	truth's nature comes forth